Moving Toward Harmony

by
Eric Oberg

Editor	Lesley Thomas
Photographer	Neal Oberg
Uke	Rupert Berk and Lesley Thomas
Book Design & Production	Ken Yu/Quicksilver
Cover Design	Ken Yu/Quicksilver

Far Eastern Press
PO Box 15412
Seattle, WA 98115

ISBN: 0-9678842-0-9
Manufactured in the USA

For Lesley

Introduction

Aikido is the way of harmony with the energy of life

Our only obstacle is fear

Aikido is an art of non-violent protection
and a form of exercise

Training encourages awareness of the internal
and external surroundings

The form is practiced so that we learn the principles
that are the foundation of the form

These are my personal reflections on the principles of Aikido

Aikido Keiko

The First Step

The first step in Aikido is developing intent

Training cultivates peace within the flow of life

The primary purpose of Aikido is to create
a structure through which you can experience
harmony and well-being

Aikido is not for fighting against evil

The intent of Aikido is to bring a positive force
into the world

Ikkyo

Ikkyo is the physical expression of the intent
to live in the flow of life

Reach out to the world and welcome life

Act with the conviction
that each small thing you do
will make a difference

Entering

The essence of entering is embodiment

First enter your own body

Begin with an awareness of the breath

Let the awareness spread through the body
and the world around you

Entering the body creates the world
in the sense that it is through the body
that you discover the world

Irimi

The physical expression of entering is *irimi*

Gently move closer to the other person

No force is used to accomplish *irimi*

As you move closer you become softer and softer
until the other person is a part of your body

Then you can move freely

The Four Directions

Be courteous
Be honest
Be thankful
Be yourself in all things and with all people

First follow form

When the form is correct
be truthful

When the truth is found
be grateful

When gratitude is genuine
you will see yourself in all things

Shihonage

Shihonage expresses the four directions

Do not confront directly

Step to the side

Add yourself to the attack
then turn to face your attacker

Learn to keep your balance
even in the gravest of circumstances

Transformation

The other person will change you

Let it happen

Out of apparent conflict will come growth

With growth you will acquire wisdom

With wisdom you become patient

With patience you can accomplish great things

Tai no henka

When you meet resistance
do not fight harder

Let the attack change you

Become the person you need to become
in order to resolve the conflict

Be flexible in the way you move
and in the way you see yourself

The Second Step

When moving forward
you may meet an obstacle

Step back and let your mind settle into the ground

As you free yourself of distraction
keep the obstacle at the edge of your awareness

Nikyo

When you meet resistance
let the feet glide backward

Fix the wrist and direct
your attacker's energy into the ground

Conspiracy

They are all out to help you

Breath together and you will understand each other

Through the breath you will understand the world

Calm your breathing and let your mind settle
into the rhythm of the universe

Kokyunage

Kokyunage is the physical realization of breath power

Bring your bodies into accord
and decide on a mutual fate

Learn to control aggression
by calming your own breathing

You do not need to focus on breathing when you move

Simply move and you will not be out of breath

The Unexpected

In some situations it is necessary
to suddenly reverse your direction
in order to achieve your goal

Never lose sight of what you really want
but approach your goal in a circular manner

When it seems that you are losing your way
you suddenly return to your original course
refreshed

Kotegaeshi

When you are touched
the attack spins you out of the way

It appears that you have lost sight of the attacker

Now
return the energy to the attacker
and neutralize the attack

Heaven and Earth

When you want to realize an idea
first send your root into the ground

When you are firmly rooted
let inspiration move you

The results will be less dramatic but more satisfying

Tenchinage

When attacked with two weapons
address them both and return them
to your attacker

Do not think of dividing the energy of the attacker

Think of making the attacker whole again

The Third Step

When you feel that you are being challenged
step into the center of the problem

Take the opposite line of reasoning

Resolve the conflict
by understanding the other side of the argument

Sankyo

If the attack continues to move toward you
step in on the other side
and firmly connect the attacker to your center

Ground the energy of the attack in a small spiral

The Pure Heart

Look into your heart each day
and find out what is important

Be honest with yourself about what you want out of life

Once you discern the answer
seek only what you need

Misogi

Aikido training is purification

Begin by cleaning your body

Then clean the dojo

Then with sincere training
you can cleanse the mind and purify the heart

The Past

Do not relive the past or try to create the future

The future and past meet in the present moment

Face the task at hand
and the past will lead you into a brighter future

Ushiro

When you are attacked from behind
turn to meet the attack with a feeling of *irimi*

When you can face any challenge
there are no *ushiro* techniques

The Turning Point

Follow the principles of Aikido
and correct your own mistakes

When you feel lost
stop looking for the path

Listen to the wind
and the storm will steer you to a safe haven

Kaeshiwaza

Kaeshiwaza is returning to the principles of Aikido

Through fighting you will defeat yourself

If you attack
you can return to the path at any moment
by losing your mind to fight

Even when you start down the wrong road
you can find your way back to the center

The Last Step

When there seems to be no solution to your problem
cut down your false self

Let your spirit rise above your situation

Then land firmly on the ground

Start over and find the simplest solution

Yonkyo

When you feel the attack is overwhelming
you must join the attack on your own position

Disappear from that spot
and cut your attacker down
as they are striking you

Address the Body

You are not here to develop the spirit

Your spirit is already developed

Address the needs and health of the body
with exercise and good nutrition

You are an embodied soul

If you deny the body you stifle the soul

The lessons you need are in the physical plane

Atemi

Aikido is a physical art

Atemi is a way of addressing the body of the attacker

You may be attacked with a weapon
but you must affect the person
not the weapon

Energy

There is no shortage of energy for the body

However
energy can become restricted by tension

If you want to have a limitless supply of energy
relax

Be active but do not try

Ki

Everybody has *ki*

Ki is unconscious energy

You cannot use it to perform tricks

You cannot direct *ki* with the mind

Simply do not interfere with *ki* and you will be powerful

Never let the mind or body stop in one place

Receiving

Learn to listen with the whole body

Accept the consequences of your actions
and the rewards of sincere training

Begin down the path and follow where it leads you

Do not wander off into the dark woods
when there is a safe path before you

Ukemi

Ukemi is the ability to accept your own body

Through *ukemi* you learn to trust your body
and your intuition

Ukemi teaches the art of not doing and not fighting

Endless Possibility

When you apply the principles of Aikido
you create infinite possibility

When there is endless possibility
there is confusion

Choose what is in your heart
and you will not be unhappy

You do not need to understand everything
with your mind

Some things can only be grasped with the heart

Stay on the path of Aikido
and find gentleness and tranquility

Takemusu Aiki

In Aikido the number of techniques is infinite

Do not try to learn all of them

It is not possible

If you decide the technique before the encounter
violence will be the result

Follow the principles of Aikido
and choose the non-violent path

The correct technique will appear

Aikido Kyoju

The *Dojo*

The place where one finds the way is just a room
with an open door

Walk in

You will find nothing special

People come and go

Students teach
Teachers learn

It seems a place where something important may happen

But the door is open
so that Aikido can escape

The Aikido Class

The teaching method in Aikido is backward

We begin at the end and proceed to the beginning

The teacher does not teach by instruction

The student does not learn by study

The teacher teaches and does not understand

The student feels and understands

Together we follow the path

It leads nowhere

The Method

In Aikido practice one person learns
while the other teaches

Uke is the teacher

Tori is the student

The teacher takes the role of *tori*

The student takes the role of *uke*

The class watches as the teacher learns from the student

The Teacher

The teacher sets an example

Always learning from each student
and welcoming the beginner

Never knowing what will happen
nor judging what has happened

A curious mind and a gentle hand

Knowing that the student will not do
as she or he is told
the teacher appears to speak

The teacher is listening

The Student

The student reflects the teacher

Trying to listen
the student tells the teacher what to do

Attacking
the student reveals weakness

Defending
another weakness appears

Defenseless
the spirit is free

The student is moved to find a voice

Breathing

Life begins with breathing

Breathe deeply

Let the tension of the day fall from the body

As the body relaxes
rediscover the senses

As the senses awaken
rediscover the world

With gratitude embrace the challenge of being alive

Each time you feel unsure
exhale without using force

Warming up

Begin with gentle movement

Allow the weight to shift

Allow the feet to move

The body is light
and the root extends into the ground

Relearn the basic movements of your body

Start each class with no knowledge

When you have nothing
add nothing and you will find the way

Ukemi

Fall forward
fall back
fall to the side
roll

The very essence of *ukemi* is embracing fearlessness

Learn to casually face the gravest danger
then easily embrace your greatest love

Remember that fear distorts perception

Witness the movement of the class

Tai no henka

A gentle introduction to each other

A gradual movement into Aikido

With no thought of fighting one can change

With no fear of failing one can move

Notice what is happening between people

Without pushing and pulling there is harmony

Without judgement there is peace

Let the spirit of *Tai no henka* find its way into each technique

Practice

Practice gives the principles form

Give everything without doing

Hear every sound without speaking

See all without judging

The forms of Aikido are contained in every human body

The techniques of Aikido are formless

Ukemi creates form

Training

In training
give the principles life

As things happen
do nothing

As people practice
accept everything

The form is contained in the other person

Tori is empty

In technique there is no control

In defense no self

Training is chaos

Aikido Inyoho

The Sun

The sun creates warmth and light

You may think of these things as good
yet when you walk into the sun
you are blinded

When you try to lead others in the direction of good
your shadow is cast upon them

The sun is power

When you follow the sun you will blind yourself
and those who follow you will know only darkness

The Moon

The moon reflects the sun and the earth

Look at the moon

The light you see is sunlight

The darkness is the earth's shadow

As you stand in cold and darkness
you can see what once blinded you

Light consumes shadow
while shadow chases light

The moon is a mirror

A mirror gives you an illusion of what you are

Look in the mirror to misunderstand the self

The Earth

The earth gives you nourishment

Earth can receive the power of the sun

Then
through the earth you can have the sun's power
and meet your own needs

You stand upon the earth and do not trust it

You look to the sun
and the moon

With everything you need beneath your feet
you never have enough

The Human Being

The sun to warm you

The earth to feed you

The moon to reveal the secrets of the sun and the earth

You are not here to follow the sun

You do not need to save the earth

There is no need to understand the moon

You are not here to fear each other

Yet
these are the things you find important

Aikido

Ai is harmony

Ki is the unknowable source of life

Do is the way

As you follow the way
it will lead to that which cannot be known

Live in harmony with the mystery of life

Aikido is not the way to power

Training will not give you nourishment

Practice will not result in knowledge

Simply do not fear that which makes you a human being

That is Aikido